JERUSALEM
PRAYERS
FOR THE
WORLD TODAY

JERUSALEM PRAYERS FOR THE WORLD TODAY

George Appleton

London SPCK

First published 1974
by S.P.C.K.
Holy Trinity Church
Marylebone Road
London NW1 4DU

Reprinted 1975 by
Church Army Press
Cowley, Oxford

SBN 281 02775 7

Contents

v

vii

Acknowledgements

Thanks are due to the following for permission to quote from copyright sources:

Darton, Longman & Todd and Doubleday & Co., Inc., New York: The Jerusalem Bible

Hodder & Stoughton and Doubleday & Co., Inc., New York: The New Testament; E. T., J. Moffat

Thomas Nelson & Sons, Ltd: Holy Bible: Revised Standard Version

Sheed & Ward, Ltd: *Zen: Way to Enlightenment*, by H. M. Enomiya-Lassalle

The Sisters of the Love of God, Oxford: *The Essential Task*, by Gilbert Shaw

Les Presses de Taizé, Taizé-Communauté, France

The author regrets that he has been unable to trace the source of the Translation of No. 27.

Preface

In most cases these prayers were not written to pray; rather they came out of prayer. I found myself concerned about some happening, some friend in need or some tension within my own spirit, and took the matter to God. After some time in waiting upon God, the concern became expressed in words, usually almost spontaneously and without any need of revision. The inarticulate groans similar to those mentioned by St Paul in Romans 8. 26, became comfortingly articulate. It would be presumptuous to claim that the Spirit was pleading through these prayers, but perhaps I may hope that he was teaching me how I ought to pray. I wrote them down at the time and I have prayed them since, some of them many times.

After some of these prayers I put the date they were written and the occasion that drew them out. For example

No. 67 (Natural Disasters) was first prayed on 21 November 1970 on learning of the disastrous floods in East Pakistan.

No. 61 was prayed after a small but painful operation.

Collect No. 48 (Human Unity) was used at the meeting of the Anglican Consultative Council at Limuru in February 1971.

No. 66 (Under Attack) was prayed after three

hours battering by a group of embittered
Palestinian exiles.

No. 23 (Separate yet Present) was inspired by a
sermon of Austin Farrer's.

No. 89 (Christ our Food) was a meditation after
reading John Marsh's commentary on St John's
Gospel, and No. 88 (Faith), a litany, after reading
Ebeling's *Nature of Faith*.

I have included a small number of prayers by
other people, prayers which have been seminal in
my own efforts to pray. Among these is one, No. 1
(Thyself Alone), by Rabia, a Moslem woman
mystic of Basrah and Jerusalem, who lived about
A.D. 800.

Another (No. 6—The Essential Task) by Father
Gilbert Shaw has sustained me in times of tension
and in temptations to lose hope.

A third, No. 25, is by Father Enomiya-Lassalle
S.J., coming out of his own deep experience of
Zen forms of meditation.

No. 42, so simple and joyous, comes from Taizé.

I have also included 'A Call to Prayer' (No. 96)
which formed part of a service of intercession for
the peace and peoples of the Middle East held in
St Paul's Cathedral in May 1970, which was
attended by Jews, Moslems, and Christians.

I have collected many prayers and been greatly

helped to pray. I have written even more prayers, some at the request of others, but many more in the way I have just described. I am now discovering that I am being helped more by silent contemplation, by holding a person or concern quietly and persistently before God, and letting him work quietly and wordlessly within my spirit.

The prayer sections numbered 90–94 describe in pedestrian words how these exercises of prayer began. As they did not issue in worded prayers, I cannot describe how they took shape, except to say that they resulted in a quiet peace, a slower tempo, and a calm assurance that the matter or the person was safe in the hands of God.

It may be that the ways in which one man tries to pray may be helpful to others learning to pray. Not all the prayers in this little book had their beginnings in Jerusalem, but most of them did, and all of them have been prayed here, between the Easters of 1969 and 1973.

G.A.

1 *Thyself Alone*

O my God,
if I worship thee in desire for heaven,
   exclude me from heaven;
If I worship thee for fear of hell,
   burn me in hell.
But if I worship thee for thyself alone,
   then withhold not from me thine eternal beauty.

(*Rabia* c. 800)

2 Gloria

Glory be to thee, O Lord God,
in the mystery of thy being,
in the creation of the universe
   and in the evolution of man,
in thine incarnation in Jesus Christ,
in the availability of thy Spirit for every man,
in all the truth, love, and goodness
   that we find in the world
in thy touch upon our souls
   and in thy will for mankind.
Glory to thee, O Lord most high.

3 *The Divine Mercy*

O my God,
I thank you for your mercy,
compounded of healing, love, forgiveness, and
grace.
May I always remember it,
  draw upon it,
  gratefully accept it,
and submit myself to its healing,
  love-engendering,
  grace-giving power.

4 *God Ineffable*

O God,
I seek to know you in prayer,
to have the joy of knowing that you are.
I know that I cannot
   objectify you,
   describe you,
   reduce you to propositions,
   but only understand by faith.
Reveal yourself to me, I pray, through the records
of Jesus Christ and through his everliving presence
within me.

5 *With all my Being*

O God,
if I do not love you with all my heart,
   with all my mind,
   with all my will, and all my life,
I shall love something else with all my being.
Save me, O God, from other gods, which are no
gods:
Save me, O God, for yourself alone,
   and I shall be safe,
   I shall be free,
   I shall be whole.

6 *The Essential Task*

Look well, O soul upon thyself
    lest spiritual ambition should mislead and blind
    thee to thy essential task to wait in quietness:
    to knock and persevere in humble faith.
Knock thou in love, nor fail to keep thy place
    before the door
    that when Christ comes,
    and not before,
    he shall open unto thee
    the treasures of his love.

(*Father Gilbert Shaw*)

7 *Seeking and Finding*

O God,
I could not begin to seek you, if you had not
sought me and made yourself known to me first.
Now I want to know you more truly, deeply, and
intuitively, and to discover more about you.
I will seek until I find,
knock at your door until you open to me,
ask until I receive
    the gift of yourself
        O God, my God.

8 *Not of Ourselves*

O Lord,
we know that we are incompetent
   to heal ourselves,
   to sanctify ourselves,
   to transfigure ourselves.
Our holiness is your action in us, through our
willingness to accept the indwelling of your Spirit.
   Heal me, Lord.
   Sanctify me, Lord.
   Transfigure me, Lord.
   Fill me, Lord.
   Direct me, Lord.
   Use me, Lord.

9 *Here am I, send Me!*

I go for love of you.
I go with love from you,
I go in love, with you.

10 *Giving and Receiving*

O Almighty God, whose blessed Son, though he
was rich, yet for our sakes became poor, that we
through his poverty might become rich,
Grant us the spirit of generous self-giving, that we
may further the work of thy Church and relieve
those that are in need.
Help us who have received so freely from thee, to
give as freely in our turn, and so share the
blessedness of giving as well as the happiness of
receiving.
We ask this in the Name of him who gave himself
for the life of the world, even thy Son, Jesus
Christ our Lord.

O Spirit of God,
set at rest the crowded, hurrying, anxious thoughts
within our minds and hearts.
Let the peace and quiet of thy presence take
possession of us.
Help us to rest, to relax, to become open and
receptive to thee.
Thou dost know our inmost spirits,
the hidden unconscious life within us,
the forgotten memories of hurts and fears,
the frustrated desires,
the unresolved tensions and dilemmas.
Cleanse and sweeten the springs of our being, that
freedom, life and love may flow into both our
conscious and hidden life.
Lord, we lie open before thee, waiting for thy
peace, thy healing, and thy Word.

Grant me, Lord,
   faith
   love
   holiness
   courage
   wisdom
   through thine own indwelling.

13 *Thy Word*

O Lord,
   awake
   attentive
   alert
   open
   ardent
   silent
   listening
      Speak, Lord,
      thy servant heareth.

Grant, dear Lord, that
    every frustration
    every criticism
    every tension
    every failure
make me more selfless,
    more holy, more loving.

Dear Lord,
   Unfaltering faith
   Imperturbable patience
   Unfailing love
   Discerning wisdom
   Quiet serenity
     today, dear Lord.

O Christ, my Lord,
You came from the Father,
You lived among men and showed them the
Father,
You went to the Father,
You are ever omnipresent with him.
In the depths of our being tell us about the Father
and lead us to him so that we may know our
Creator, our Father and your Father, your God
and our God, ever-loving and ever-loved,
ever-blessing and ever-blessed, to whom be all the
love of our hearts and the devotion of our worship,
now and always.

O God, let me follow Jesus of Nazareth in simplicity and faith.

Let him be such a part of my life that my attitudes, my thinking and behaviour may be based on him.

May I know him so intimately that I may speak of him naturally and happily.

Help me to be his follower—in every part of my life and in every day of my life, for his sake and for my own sake.

18 *Christification*

Strengthen, O Lord,
the progress of Christification
in the spirits of men,
by new insights of truth,
further impulses to goodness,
growing maturity within,
a deeper, wider love of our fellow-men,
as well as by our willed communion with you and
our experience of your Spirit at work in our
spirits,
so that we may grow to the true humanity seen in
Jesus Christ, our Lord.

O Christ, my fellow-man,
let me walk with you and see my humanity in the
light of yours,
recognizing the subtle evasiveness and the hidden
crookedness of my own soul,
and the disguised self-interested motives.
Let me be a fool of love with you.
And let me hope for myself,
because you still hope in me.

O Lord Christ,
ever-living and ever-present,
make known to me the ways of God and his
purpose in human history.
Interpret to me the meaning of your own incarnate
life, and the experience of your earliest disciples.
Open my eyes to see you working unrecognized
with men of good will who seek truth and practise
the virtue they know.
Make relevant to my life and the world in which
I live, the truth about yourself.
Let me have something of your mind and heart and
character, and infuse into me your Spirit to be my
light, my life, my love, my strength.
O Lord Christ,
ever-living, ever-present.

Never Enough

Lord,
I can never love thee enough,
    never thank thee enough,
    never serve thee enough.
Be thou my sufficiency,
    that inspired by thee,
    I may do good things,
    loving things,
and strengthened by thee,
    do difficult things,
    attempt impossible things,
in thee and for thee
    O Lord, my God.

22 *The True Cross*

O Christ, my Lord,
You tell me that I am to take up my cross and
follow you.
Help me to know that it is a cross laid on me by
you, and not a cross of my own, made by lack of
holiness or love.
If it is a true cross, grant me acceptance, quiet
trust in you, and courage.
If it is of my own making, make me see the cause
which produced it,
and nail the old self to it,
so that dying with you,
I may have your risen life,
your values,
your attitudes,
your desire for the Father's will,
and your obedience to it,
O Lord of all true crosses.

23 *Separate yet Present*

O thou who art utterly separate in being and
entirely present in love, attach our minds, hearts
and wills to thee.
Help us to look with thine eyes and to care with
thy heart, to have thy compassion for evil and thy
delight in good; to stand in thy uncreated light
and to reflect the light from the face of him, who
is thy brightness, Jesus Christ, our Lord.

I have calmed and quieted my soul, like a child
quieted at its mother's breast,
   like a child that is quieted
     is my soul.

Psalm 131 (*RSV*)

I wait for the Lord, my soul waits,
   and in his word I hope; .
   my soul waits for the Lord
more than watchmen for the morning
more than watchmen for the morning.

Psalm 130

Leave it all quietly to God, my soul,
   my rescue comes from him alone;
     rock, rescue, refuge,
       he is all to me.

Psalm 62 (*Moffatt*)

25 *Christ Within*

O Christ my Lord, I pray that you will turn my
heart to you in the depths of being, where with
the noise of creatures silenced and the clamour of
bothersome thoughts stilled, I shall stay with you,
where I find you always present and where I love
and worship you.

(Father H. M. Enomiya-Lassalle S.J.)

26 *Inner Holiness*

Keep me, O Lord,
ever dependent on you,
holy and loving,
humble and trusting,
courageous in faith,
reverent and worshipping,
forgetful of self,
wanting only your will and your glory,
through Jesus Christ my Lord.

27 *Holy Desires*

Desire to have pleasure in nothing
Desire to possess nothing
Desire to know nothing
Desire to be nothing
    in order to have everything
        in Christ.

(*St John of the Cross*)

28 *Gratitude for our Calling*

O God we thank thee for our birth,
for thy care for us until now,
for thy choice of us,
    thy call to us,
    thy hope in us,
for thy promise to us of love, grace, strength,
the fullness of the Spirit of Jesus Christ,
thine incarnate Son,
our Saviour and our Lord.

29 *The Single Eye*

Grant me, O Lord, the single eye, that I may see
the one thing needful,
the thing that you want done.
Don't let my vision be blurred by looking at too
many things or trying to please anyone but you.
Give me simplicity of heart, quiet confidence in
you, and eagerness to know and do your will,
like your beloved Son,
Jesus Christ,
my beloved Brother and Lord.

30 *Sins*

O God,
I recognize that my sins are
spiritual sickness,
selfishness,
incompleteness,
immaturity,
lack of faith,
falling short of your Will and your Glory.
Let your grace heal me,
make me selfless,
lead me to maturity and holiness,
complete me,
according to the pattern of
your unique Son,
Jesus Christ, my Lord.

31 *A Consuming Fire*

O Holy Spirit,
help me to submit to thy fire,
that all that is not holy may be burnt,
and all that is not eternal may be destroyed.
Help me to hold myself in thy fire,
until all that is foreign is consumed,
and I burn with the bright painless flames
of holiness and love.

Thy will be done:
  So good
  So holy
  So loving
  So wise
  So effective
    Thy will be done!

O my God
    I still have a lust
    to be always right,
    to be seen to be right.
Let me desire only
    thy will.
    Let it be done,
    in hiddenness,
    in trusted rightness,
    in spite of frequent failure,
        humbly, lovingly, joyfully.

34 *Immediate and Total*

Complete trust in thee
Immediate reference to thee
Utter dependence on thee
   Always, O blessed Lord.

35 *New Being*

O my Lord and Friend,
you are constantly with me.
You are infinitely stronger,
more holy, more loving,
more wise than I am.
Take the lead, dear Lord,
guide me,
fashion me,
strengthen me,
sanctify me,
make me loving.
I put myself in your hands without reserve.
Let me be, and do, and bear all
that is your will for me.

36 *Signs*

Lord, I thank thee for so many signs that you are
at work:
    in people whom I meet,
    in people you send to me,
    in everything that happens,
unbaring the spiritual realities
    in men's longing for peace,
    in new clues to peace,
    in people of other faiths,
    in growing emptiness, openness, and serenity,
Dear Lord, I thank you.

37 *Holding On*

O God,
I bring this situation to thee and hold it to thee,
refusing to let it get away from thee,
believing that by thy grace,
in answer to my prayer
it will change,
that something will turn up
that was not there before,
that the mountain of difficulty will be removed
or thy wisdom show me the way to go round
or thy grace strengthen me to climb over it
or tunnel through it.
Let me hold on in faith and love,
O Lord my God.

38 *In Controversy*

Lord, give me
   deep understanding,
   unfailing patience,
   gentle meekness,
   truth with love,
   salt in speech,
   expectant faith,
   dogged persistence,
and above all,
   the mind of Christ.

O thou who through countless ages hast seen the
follies of men and their upward strivings and hopes,
Guide us by thy ever-growing hindsight in the
ways of righteousness and love. Grant that from
the knowledge of man's success and failure in the
past we may be guided by wisdom as we continue
the upward journey to the goal which is thy will
for both the universe and mankind,
O Creator and Saviour of all, from the beginning,
now and to all eternity.

A Morning Prayer

Abba, Father,
I thank you for bringing me to today,
for all the blessings of the past,
for my birth, parents, and home, for family and
friends and all who have helped to train me for life,
and for all your grace.
I thank you for yesterday, for the good things that
happened and for your help in the problems,
difficulties and temptations.
I bring today to you for your guidance and
blessing.
Help me to discover your will and to follow it
trustingly, faithfully, and gratefully,
like your beloved Son,
my dear Master and Lord,
Jesus Christ.

O Lord my God,
I bring to you the duties already arranged
for today
. . . .
guide and strengthen me for each.
There are other things, O Lord, which will come
to me today unplanned by me:
visitors, letters, telephone calls,
unforeseen happenings.
Let me be so aware of your abiding presence with
me,
that I may respond to each in dependence on you,
asking your will,
infused with your love and
strengthened by your grace,
O blessed Lord.

42 *Today*

Keep us, O Lord, today in the
    joy
    simplicity
    and compassionate love
of the gospel.

(*Taizé*)

43 *A Nightly Thanksgiving*

O God, I thank thee
for thy goodness
thy beauty
thy love
and for thyself.
I thank thee
for the world
for life
for friends and colleagues
and for today
. . . .

Thanks, blessing, and glory to thee, my Lord,
with the love of my heart.
And praise for Jesus, thy unique Son,
through whom I have come to know thee
and to call thee Father.

O Lord,
in all the problems, difficulties, misgivings, and
uncertainties, I look in trust to you, asking for
your insight and guidance.
Show me things to do now which will create new
possibilities, develop dedicated personalities,
deepen fellowship.
Let me never presume to worry for you,
but be quietly confident that you are working in
your Church and in individual souls,
O Lord of the Church,
O Master of every disciple,
O Lover of every soul.

45 *Within and Without*

O Holy Spirit of God,
You are giving me courage to trust my inner
experiences and intuitions.
Let me open my whole being to your incarnation
in me and be conscious of your presence ever
surrounding me,
O immediate, ever-present Lord.

46 'Isness' and Becoming

O Creator Lord,
let me feel the 'isness' of things and people,
without resistance,
without trying to impose my own pattern upon
them
or exploit them for selfish ends.
Let me welcome them,
enjoy them,
value them,
love them,
for what they are and for what they are becoming
through your creative love.

O God, to know you is life eternal,
to serve you is perfect freedom. Grant that I may
know you more truly, more intimately, more
clearly, and serve you in freedom, with courage and
flame, in all my days, through Jesus Christ, my
Lord.

48 *Human Unity*

O God who hast made of one blood all nations
of the earth, and didst send thy blessed Son to be
the redeemer of all mankind: Unite us in our
common humanity and make us one new man in
the same thy Son, Jesus Christ, our Lord.

Grant, O Lord, that as the light from the farthest
star comes to our sight through millions of light
years, so may the light from the Star of Bethlehem
shine through millions of light years ahead to the
eyes of faith, directing men to the Eternal Word
who speaks to every generation of thee, and thy
love and thy truth,
even our incarnate Lord,
Jesus Christ.

50 *Transfiguration*

Let the divine spark in me kindle into flame,
O Christ my Lord,
that radiance and warmth may shine through my
whole being, and show that I have been with thee
on the mountain of glory.

O Christ,
who didst call James to be a fisher of men,
to be one of the intimate three and to be the first
apostle to give his life in death,
Grant us to know thee more intimately,
to catch men so that they may know thy grace
and love,
and to show in life or in death that we are thy
intimate friends and faithful followers.
We ask this in loving trust,
O Lord and Master.

Lord,
give me deeper faith in thee within my own being,
greater trust and confidence in the insights and
guidance that come from thee,
deeper thankfulness for all thy love and grace,
O thou who art my Lord and my all.

Grant, O Lord,
that I may not fail thee
   in the moment of truth,
      of temptation,
      of crisis,
      of opportunity.

Lord,
I am not a fraction of what I am meant to be in
thy divine will,
not a fraction of what I can become through thy
grace.

Psalm 43.3

Send out your light and your truth,
  let these be my guide,
to lead me to your holy mountain
  and to the place where you live.

56 Death

We are all mortal, O Lord,
and our future lies with thee.
Make us so conscious of thee that death may be no
break but a deeper dimension of being.
Help us to leave no duty undone,
no sin unrepented,
no relationship unsanctified,
and grant us the faith that the best is yet to be.
So let us live in hope and love,
without fear and without regret,
knowing thee to be the God and Father of
Jesus Christ and ours.

O Lord God,
Thou knowest how much the souls of the departed
need thy forgiveness and cleansing before they are
ready to feel at home in thy presence.
Grant that in the clearer light of Paradise they
may see their need,
and accept the grace and love which thou hast ever
offered them since the moment of their creation.
So most gracious God, Thou wilt be to them their
Redeemer as well as their Creator,
and all through Jesus Christ, our Lord.

O Christ,
the little girl on her deathbed,
the young man on the way to his grave,
and Lazarus three days in the tomb,
could all hear your voice.
May each soul as it passes through death, hear your
friendly voice,
see the look of love in your eyes
and the smile of welcome in your face,
and be led by you to the Father of all souls.

59 *Time and Eternity*

O thou who art unlimited by the laws of time and
space under which we thy creatures live;
Grant that we may so love and serve thee in time
that we may be found worthy to enjoy thee in
eternity,
who art the source and goal of all,
ever to be worshipped in the mystery of thy Being,
blessed from the beginning,
blessed now and blessed
for evermore.

Grant, O Lord,
that the years that are left
may be the holiest,
the most loving,
the most mature.
I thank you for the past and especially that you
have kept the good wine until now.
Help me to accept diminishing powers as the
opportunity to prepare my soul for the full and
free life to come in the state prepared by your Son,
Jesus Christ, our Lord.

61 *In Pain*

The worst of pain, O Lord, is that it makes it
difficult to pray.
Yet, O Lord, I desire to pray, to have communion
with you, to draw strength and healing from you,
to link to you those whom I love and those who
need your love,
to thank you for those who look after me and
those who wish me well.
O Lord, let me always remember that to talk to
you is prayer.

62 *For the Sick*

Almighty and Merciful God, Creator and
Redeemer,
we bring before thee all who are sick in body,
mind, or spirit.
Let them feel secure in thy love, and know that
with thy grace all shall be well, in sickness or in
health, in life or in death,
through Jesus Christ, our Lord.

63 The Divine Omniscience and Mercy

O thou who art everywhere present and dost know
the secrets of all hearts and the frustrating griefs
and sins of men and nations, communicate thy
insights to all who work for peace that we may
know how to interpret, heal, plead, and find the
way to the peace of thine omniscient will,
O Creator, Judge, and Redeemer of all.

Guide our feet into the way of peace,
for in our confusion we do not know which way
to turn,
in the babel of voices we hear no clear word,
in the mass of propaganda we cannot find the
truth.
Give us direction in which to move, and when we
cannot find it
guide our feet by thy wisdom, if unperceived by
our understanding.
Keep our hearts peaceful in trust,
give us quiet courage,
keep us steady under criticism or opposition,
with unfailing love towards all, and eager
expectation to see the footmarks of thy dear Son
ahead, perhaps only a step or two, but pointing
to the peace of thy will,
O Creator and Redeemer of all.

O God, I thank thee
for unexpected encouragement,
for people who come in unforeseen ways,
for changes in positions which seem hopelessly
hardened.
I know now, O Lord, that thou art always at work
where truth seems threatened,
human wisdom exhausted,
good will missing.
Remind me, ever-present Spirit, when my faith and
hope are low, of these evidences of thy activity in
the past, and let me watch with eager interest for
thy intervention.
Keep me steady and alert,
ever ready to respond and obey,
O thou Lord of ever-ruling providence.

66 *Under Attack*

O God, grant that when under attack or
criticism I may stand before thee in a spirit of
integrity, wanting only the truth of each situation
and thy will to respond to it.
O Lord, I know that I can never expect complete
certainty, but can only act in faith.
I know that if I act in faith and move forward in
what I believe is thy will, thou canst direct me and
correct my course if it be wrong.
If I am paralysed in fear, thou canst not guide me.
Let me fear nothing except to be faithless to thee;
nor let me be consciously defensive;
nor hit back on those who attack;
nor become bitter or self-pitying;
nor fail in the desire for truth and the expression
of unfailing good will.
For the sake of him who came to bear witness to
thy truth and embodied thy truth and love,
even Jesus Christ, my Lord.

67 *Natural Disasters*

O God of goodness,
in the mystery of natural disasters we look to thee,
trusting that there is an explanation that will
satisfy our minds and hearts.
Accept our compassion for our fellow-men,
our desire for their relief,
and our hope for knowledge which shall control
the forces of nature.
Help us to help thee to complete thy universe,
O Creator Father,
to remove its flaws,
so that we may be sub-creators with thee of the
Kingdom of thy love in Jesus Christ.

68 *The Casualties of History*

O God,
my mind and spirit fail in the thought of all the
casualties of history:
those who have died in war,
in famine, in natural disasters,
in the harshness and injustice of men,
in diseases as yet incurable,
in heartache, loneliness, and despair.
If thou art not a God of mercy, redemption and
love, my pain is incurable.
But I am comforted in the thought that the
creature cannot rise higher than his Creator,
my love is only a tiny fraction of thine.
I thank thee for him who came from thy heart to
speak to mine, even Jesus Christ.

Grant us to look with thine eyes of compassion,
O merciful God, at the long travail of mankind:
the wars, the hungry millions,
the countless refugees,
the natural disasters,
the cruel and needless deaths,
men's inhumanity to one another,
the heartbreak and hopelessness of so many lives.
Hasten the coming of the messianic age
when the nations shall be at peace,
and men shall live free from fear and free from
want
and there shall be no more pain or tears,
in the security of thy will
and the assurance of thy love,
shown us in Jesus the Christ, the Saviour of all.

O God,
Your divine consciousness can hold all creation
and all eternity in a timeless moment.
Your compassion can bear all the sorrows of men
and tragedies of history.
Your love can embrace every living and departed
soul.
I am but a microscopic miniature of you.
Keep me true to the divine likeness that loving and
compassioning to my full measure, I may trust all
to your infinite love and mercy, which surpass all
we know and all we can desire.

71 *Armistice Day*

May the memory of two world wars strengthen
our efforts for peace,
May the memory of those who died inspire our
service to the living,
May the memory of past destruction move us to
build for the future,
O Father of souls,
O God of peace,
O Builder of the Kingdom.

O Lord Christ,
ever-living and ever-present,
Make known to me the ways of God and his
purpose in human history,
Interpret to me the meaning of your own incarnate
life and the experience of your earliest disciples,
Help me to see you working anonymously with
men of good will, who seek truth and practise the
virtue they know, and serve their fellow men.
Make relevant to my life and the world in which I
live, the truth about yourself.
Let me have something of your mind and character
and heart, and infuse into me your Spirit to be my
light, my life, my strength and love,
O Lord Christ, ever-living, ever-present.

O Christ,
I used to think I had
to keep seeking,
to keep asking,
to keep knocking
until you responded.
Now I know that I have
only to seek and I shall find,
only to ask and you will answer,
only to knock and your door will at once be
opened.
You do not demand importunity but simply faith,
O gracious, self-giving Lord.

Give me your love for them.
Help me to help them find your will.
Save me from playing God to them.
Let me be your messenger if you need one.
Let me be a friend-in-you to them,
as loving,
understanding,
patient,
non-judgemental,
as you are,
as hopeful as you are.
Do for them, O Father, in Christ Jesus,
all that they need.

75 *Insight*

O Lord,
help me to see into the souls of men:
their needs, their fears, their hopes, their sickness
of soul,
the causes of their restlessness.
Help me to see what they can become by your
grace,
encouraged by my understanding.
Lord Jesus, give me this kind of sight:
    to look, to see
    to understand, to pity,
    to love, to heal.

O my Lord,
let me not be censorious, judgemental, negative.
Let me understand and identify myself with my
fellow men.
Let me be open to their 'isness' and hopeful for
their becoming and my own,
under your gentle, firm, creative hands.

O Lord, let the Church be truly your collective
body in the world today, the Christ-Community
directed by you its Head, infused with your
Spirit, loving and serving men as you did when
you lived our human life.

Help the Church to give itself for the world, so
that men may have the priceless treasure of your
grace and love, O Lord of the Church, O Saviour
of the world.

O God, I go pushed by you.
I will go willingly, eagerly, expectantly,
hoping to learn deeper truth,
to see more of your world purpose,
to share other men's experience of you,
to give something if you have already given it to
me.
Prepare me, O Spirit of God, and all with whom
I go,
that we may be grasped, inspired, and transformed
more deeply and consciously by you,
for his sake.

Grant, O Father
that I may be a father-in-you to all under my care,
that I may speak your word to all among whom
    I live,
that I may be a healer-in-Christ to all who are ill,
    in spirit, mind or body,
that I may be a friend to all whom I meet,
that I may love your world and rejoice in its
    wonder,
that I may see you at work in the world, in events,
    in people and in myself;
for Jesus' sake
your unique beloved Son
and my beloved brother and Lord.

O God of Abraham, Isaac, and Jacob, Grant that
Israel of today may inherit the callings and
blessings of Israel of old.
May it be
 a God-ruled nation within itself
 a nation of priests to the world
 a blessing to all nations
 a joy to the whole earth.
Revive, O Lord God,
 the gift of prophecy
 the perception of your will
 the speaking of your Word.
Deepen, O Lord,
 a sense of responsibility for the world
 the care for the stranger, the homeless and the
  poor
 the consciousness of your judgement.
Let it look afresh
 to its son Jesus of Nazareth
 to the Church which developed from itself
 to all its Semitic brethren
 to the House of Islam sharing in some degree
  its faith in you.
So that it may accomplish
 your purpose for the world and for itself.
O Holy One of Israel,
O God of all.

81 *For Jerusalem*

O Eternal Lord God, Source of all truth, Lover of
all men, we thank thee for the experience of living
in this city.

Grant that we may be humble, grateful people,
  worshipping people,
  holy people.

Help us to be peace-loving people,
  who know the things that belong to peace,
  who pray and work for peace,
  who try to understand the experiences, the
    hurts, the hopes of people from whom we
    differ.

Let this city be a centre of unity for the Churches.

Let it be a place of friendship and understanding
  for men of different faiths.

Let it be truly the City of Peace, a joy of the
  whole earth and a place of blessing to all nations.

For the sake of him who wept in love over this
  city and died in love outside its walls.

Now the Everliving One, ever present with thee
  to heal and bless, Jesus Christ our blessed Lord
  and Saviour.

82 *The Messianic Age*

Let the time come, O God, when there shall be
peace on earth, brotherhood among races, freedom
from fear and freedom from want, freedom to
think and speak at the dictates of conscience, when
our systems of justice shall be protective and
healing, when people shall live in Christ's way in a
world closer to the principles of thy Kingdom.
We ask this in the name of him who inaugurated
this kingdom and was its first citizen, Jesus the
Christ.

O Christ,
Lord of the Church,
you founded your Church to take to all men the
good news brought by you from God;
you want it to be a servant community to the
world,
and to gather all men into the divine love:
Grant that we your servants in the Jerusalem
Archbishopric may fulfil these purposes of love;
sanctify us,
fill us with love,
and prepare us to accept these responsibilities, in
fellowship with our sister Churches throughout
the world,
O Lord of the Churches,
O Saviour of men.

84 *With all my Being*

O Lord my God, let me love you
with all my being,
with all my mind, my thinking, my desire and
search for truth,
with all my heart, with all my feeling,
with my desire and longing, in every mood, in
every circumstance,
with all my life, all day and every day, until life
shall end, in every happening, every relationship,
with all my will, in every choice, every decision,
every intention, every effort, in all my faltering,
wanting only your holy, righteous, loving will.
So loving you, with all my being, I shall have the
life which you alone can give,
strengthened by him whose delight was to do
your will,
who has brought me to you,
even Jesus Christ, my Lord.

OPEN

to everything and everyone,
no rejection,
no pre-judgement,
no resistance,
to what happens,
to privations, diminishments.
Open to the 'isness' of things,
not defensive,
ready to admit others into myself.
Open, above all, to your Spirit
Never closed or final.
Open to believe that you can change people and
reveal the real factors.

PLIANT

no rigidity,
no legalistic spirit,
ready to give without giving way,
accepting the impact of others,
humble,
patient,
receptive,
resilient,
hopeful.

FREE
from self, ambition, fear,
dislike of criticism,
fear of making a mistake,
fear of responsibility.

Give me the freedom of the Spirit, which frees me
from all lesser loyalties, and from all that holds me
back from the divine will.

EAGER

glad acceptance, because you are
so good,
so loving,
so wise,
so sovereign,
so ready to direct, strengthen, enlighten.

Not just acceptance and obedience—but glad
expectation ... Joy ...

And eagerness that is willing to wait because it
knows the end, yet looking for initiative.

Yes! Lord, Yes!
Open ... Pliant ... Free ... Eager ...
Yes! Lord, Yes! Always yes!

Abba, Father, my Father, our Father.
Father of our Lord Jesus Christ,
Father of all,
Pattern of all fatherhood;
Father, dear Father,
Perfection and prototype of all fatherhood.

Father in heaven,
the sphere of the spiritual and eternal,
of perfection, holiness, blessing and love,
not far removed, but omnipresent,
perceptible to the eyes of faith,
tangible to the action of faith.

May I know you more deeply,
more intimately, more truly,
know you as seen in Jesus Christ,
both in his incarnate life and in his incarnation
within ourselves.
May I reverence and love you,
may all do so.

May I love you with all my heart,
with all my mind,
with all my will and in the depths of my being.
May no lesser loyalties rule over me.
May your rule deepen in me and extend over the
world in which we live.

May your righteous, loving, holy, effective will be
done in me and in the world, by me and by
growing numbers of people—the loveliest, most
perfect, passing all understanding and all desire.

On earth as in the spiritual sphere,
by me as by the angels and saints, here and now,
approximating more closely to the perfection with
which your unique Son Jesus obeyed and
effected it.

Hasten the time when all men shall have sufficient
food and all that is necessary for abundant living.
Give me spiritual food for today, for its duties,
its difficulties, its opportunities, and adventures.

Forgive my selfishness,
my immaturity,
my failing in love,
my timidities and lack of faith,
my falling short of all that I can become by your
grace.
Heal all the diseases of my soul,
make up all my deficiencies.

May I learn that I only remain within the circle of
your forgiveness, if I too forgive anyone who has
harmed me.
Save me from being self-righteous, censorious,
judgemental.

Make me understanding and compassionate
towards all who sin.

Don't let me fall into temptation
through weakness, self-will, pride,
the memory of past falls,
the persuasion of others,
or the prevailing assumptions of the world around
me.

Alert me to evil,
don't let it get any entry into mind, imagination, will.
Protect me, save me,
from evil without or within.
Sanctify me, fill me with love.
For all belongs to you.
You have made all,
You love all,
You will to save all and to bring all men into your
Kingdom of righteousness and love.
And it is only through your faithful love that we
continue to live,
only through your power that we are strong,
only through your grace that we grow in maturity
and holiness.
So the glory is yours,
for all that is and all that can become.
Glory be to you, Creator, Saviour, Lord,
Our Father, for ever and ever.

O Spirit of the Lord, grant me

UNDERSTANDING

insight into the meaning of things,
the significance of happenings,
the needs, the hopes, the motives of people.

WISDOM

to know what ought to be done,
what can be done,
the obstacles which must be surmounted before
    your will can be done,
wisdom also to know the right time to act.

COUNSEL

Your insight and guidance,
so that I may be creative and helpful, resourceful,
never without hope in you and in men,
never defeated or negative.

POWER

strength to stand in the day of doubt, difficulty
    or despair,
strength to be quick to decision when sudden
    action is needed,

to sustain me in time of pressure,
to keep going trustingly in days of routine and
   waiting.

KNOWLEDGE

to know all that needs to be known,
all that can be known,
to trace the course of past events, to connect cause
   and effect, to understand all the factors involved,
   and above all to know you intimately and
   lovingly.

GODLINESS

to be truly your child and servant,
to have your mind and character,
to be like you,
to do things in your way,
to see the world and men through your eyes of
   love, compassion, and righteousness.

HOLY FEAR

the loving reverence of a son,
who fears lest he should fail his Father,
grieve him by sinfulness or fear or self-will,
always eager to understand and obey.

91

O Spirit of God,
let your Spirit rest upon me,
upon the Church,
upon mankind:

For the sake of him on whom your Spirit descended
in all his fullness, Jesus Christ, my Lord.

Faith is believing see-ing, in-seeing, insight,
spiritual sight.
Lord, that I may receive my sight.

Faith is the way in which God is apprehended, it
is seeing him who is invisible.
Lord, show me the Father.

Believing is not a thing, it is an event, something
which happens.
Let thy loving mercy come unto me O Lord.

To believe is to depend solely on God; I come to
him empty-handed.
My sufficiency is from thee, O God.

Faith is a choice, a decision—about where a man
is, where he is at home.
Lord, let me abide with thee.

Faith is waiting for the Word of God, the key to
each situation, which heals the past, copes with the
present, and opens up the future
*My soul waits for thee, O Lord and in thy word I
trust.*

I can do without everything but the Lord: the one
who is absolutely necessary to me is God
Lord, apart from thee, I can do nothing.

Faith lets the future approach. It creates the future from the present. It wrestles with the present to gain from it a blessing for the future
It is thee, O Lord, I will not be afraid.

Faith sets the believer free—free from guilt, free from care, free from fear, free from constricting limitation, free from the opinions or opposition or inertia of others, free to go forward and act.
Lord, if thou set me free, I shall be truly free.

Faith is present when looking at the most difficult situation it says 'Nevertheless'.
Nevertheless, at thy Word, O my Lord.

Faith is most faith when it is tempted and threatened, when in the face of every misgiving and reverse, it continues to say 'My God!'
Lord, I believe, help thou my unbelief.

Faith is never impatient. For faith every moment is right.
Lord, I have learned in whatever state I am to be content.

Jesus is the author and perfector of my faith. He makes faith possible both by his incarnate life and by his continuing presence.
I know him when I have believed.

Faith is to participate in Jesus and in his way, to share in the power of God who raised him from the dead.

Lord, share with me thy risen life.

Faith is not the pre-condition of salvation, but the assurance of it.

O my God, I will give thanks unto thee for ever.

89 *John 6: Christ our Food*

A profound parable of God's nourishing of the soul.

Jesus is the satisfaction of the inner hunger that men experience.

He gives the real food that a man needs for his inner life.

This food cannot be earned as men earn their daily bread. It is a gift—from God in Christ.

'He who eats me, comes to me, is united to me, follows me, learns from me, is guided by me, lives in my mileu, lets me live in him, lives by me, draws strength from me;

this man receives spiritual nourishment, which gives life, health, staying power.'

I can share Christ's life, the life that was offered in death and came triumphantly through death.

When I participate in Christ, I participate in the power of God who raised him from the dead.

The food which Christ supplies will keep me going through every difficulty, every temptation, every illness, every misfortune, every opportunity, every adventure, through the birth of death as I pass from the material and temporal, into the spiritual and eternal.

Lord, give me this bread always.

IN THREE STEPS

1. On the lips, said aloud, perhaps twenty or more times.
2. In the mind, attention held on the Name.
3. In the heart, at the centre of the being, with the mind now quiet.

NAMES

Abba
Jesus
Saviour
Lord
Spirit of Wisdom
Spirit of Holiness
Spirit of Love

Repeated slowly many times, then silently many times, allowing the meaning to deepen into feeling, holding the attention on the text whenever it strays away, until at last the mind is silent and I experience the truth or the promise of which the text speaks.

TEXTS:

Peace I leave with you, my peace I give unto you.

Come unto me, all ye who labour and are heavy laden, and I will refresh you.

It is I, be not afraid.

Abide in me and let me abide in you.

My grace is sufficient for you.

Underneath are the everlasting arms.

I am with you always.

In quietness and confidence shall be your strength.

I have made, and I will bear.

Your ears shall hear a word behind you, saying, This is the way, walk in it.

Holding a name lovingly, trustingly before God,
without diagnosing the person's need,

or telling God what to do,

leaving God to do what in his love he knows to be
most needed.

The name may be repeated many times,
on the lips or in the mind,
and then, held silently in the heart.

If our Lord's name is added after the name of the
one for whom we are praying,
his love is invoked to magnify our own human
love.

93 *The Radiating Prayer*

Beginning from within the heart, and sending out
to those near to us,
then in widening circles to others
in our village or town,
to those of our own nation,
then neighbouring nations,
till finally the whole of mankind, living and
departed, is reached in the radiation in turn of
goodwill,
> compassion,
> love,
> joy,
> peace,
> blessing,

remembering that these lovely dispositions start
from God within ourselves and are reinforced by
his infinitely more generous radiation.

The Jesus Prayer

Lord Jesus Christ, Son of God,
have mercy on me, a sinner.

In this prayer, one of the great treasures of the
Orthodox Church, the words 'have mercy'
(*eleison* in Greek) come from the same root as
elaion olive tree and the oil from it. So they speak
of healing, soothing, grace.

Each word or phrase in the prayer should be
dwelt upon and its meaning allowed to penetrate
through the mind to the heart which is the centre
of being.

Lord ... Jesus ... Christ ... Son of God ...
heal, strengthen, forgive ... me ... a sinner

—repeated slowly, recollectedly, lovingly ...
silently, deeply, gratefully.

95 *An Easter Blessing*

May the love of the cross,
the power of the resurrection,
and the presence of the Living Lord,
be with you always.
And the blessing of the
Eternal God,
Creator and Father,
Risen Lord and Saviour,
Giver of holiness and love
be upon you now and evermore.

(Part of a service of intercession in St Paul's Cathedral for the peace and peoples of the Middle East)

I wish I could sound this call to prayer in the moving way in which it is sounded five times a day in the muezzin call from the minaret, or with the impressive sense of worship with which the cantor in the synagogue would voice it. The little I can bring is the deep feelings of one heart that tries to hold Jews, Muslims, and Christians, Arabs, and Israelis in a tension of love.

We come together before our Creator, the Sovereign Lord of the Universe, the Lord of Righteousness and Compassion, the God of peace and love, as his children, all of us in one way or another children of Abraham, the Father of the faithful, to offer ourselves as instruments of understanding, healing, and reconciliation, to be channels of his love and grace through our prayers.

I move about, by the kind understanding of governments, through all the countries of the Middle East. I have not met a single person who does not desperately long for peace.

I ask you to pray that God will give us in addition to this desire for peace the will for peace. This can be generated and deepened by trying to understand what is going on in the soul of the Arab, and equally to try and find out what is going on in the soul of the Jew.

I ask you to pray that God will show us the way to peace, that he will inspire some leader, thinker, statesman, man of faith, with a divine clue which will lead to some initiative towards peace.

I ask you to pray that he will give us a vision of the Middle East, of the whole world, a vision of what is in his will, which will lift us to new hope, faith, obedience, and love.

Let us pray in a way that holds close to God the land which we all love, the city which we all call holy, with all its problems, griefs, hatreds, and fears, believing that when we pray with loving persistence, God will work with unfailing love. Pray that we who live there may be holy people to make a holy city and a holy land.

This call is not an appeal for just one evening in the year, but for every day of the year. Let me end with a word from Isaiah, a prophet whom Muslims, Jews, and Christians all revere:

You who are the Lord's remembrancers, take no rest, and give him no rest, until he establishes Jerusalem and makes it a praise in the earth,

We don't have to importune God, as if he were

unwilling. He is more ready to hear than we to pray. He gives more than we deserve, praised be his holy Name for that, more even than we desire.

So, let us pray.

Jerusalem:
The rock of Abraham's faith, where he was willing
to offer his only son.

V. My father, behold the fire and the wood, but
   where is the lamb?
R. *God will provide himself the lamb, my son.*

Jerusalem:
The City of David, the shepherd king, the singer
of Israel's psalms of praise.

V. Praise the Lord O my soul;
R. *And all that is within me praise His holy Name.*

Jerusalem:
Where Solomon built the Temple for the worship
of God.

V. I was glad when they said unto me;
R. *We will go into the House of the Lord*

Jerusalem:
Where sacrifice was offered for the forgiveness of
sins.

V. This is a true saying and worthy to be received
   by all men;
R. *That Christ Jesus came into the world to save
   sinners.*

Jerusalem:
Where the infant Jesus was offered to God in the Temple.

V. A light to the nations;
R. *And the glory of Israel*

Jerusalem:
Where the boy Jesus lingered in his Father's House.

V. O lover of children;
R. *Bless the children of our Jerusalem*

Jerusalem:
The City over which Jesus wept.

V. How often would I have gathered thy children;
R. *O Jerusalem! Jerusalem!*

Jerusalem:
Not knowing the things that belong to peace.

V. We pray for thy peace;
R. *O Jerusalem! Jerusalem!*

Jerusalem:
With the Upper Room where Jesus washed his disciples' feet; where he instituted the remembrance of his death and gave the new commandment to love as he loves.

V. Verily I say, one of you shall betray me;
R. *Lord is it I? Is it I?*

Jerusalem:
With Gethsemane on the Mount of Olives.

V. By thine agony and bloody sweat;
R. *Have mercy on us.*

Jerusalem:
With the pavement where Jesus was condemned.

V. Father forgive them;
R. *For they know not what they do.*

Jerusalem:
With the hill of crucifixion outside the city wall.

V. God commends his love toward us;
R. *Because while we were still sinners Christ died
   for us.*

Jerusalem:
With the garden of resurrection glory.

V. I am the Living One, I was dead
R. *Behold I am alive for evermore.*

Jerusalem:
Oft destroyed by foreign armies but rising again.

V. We pray for thy peace;
R. *O Jerusalem! Jerusalem!*

Jerusalem:
With the ancient wall where Jewish brethren
lament, rejoice, and pray.

V. O pray for the peace of Jerusalem;
R. *May they prosper that love thee.*

Jerusalem:
Mistakenly fought for by Crusader armies.

V. Blessed are the peacemakers;
R. *For they are the children of God.*

Jerusalem:
Longed for by exiles of many generations.

V. Jerusalem that is above;
R. *The mother of us all.*

Jerusalem:
Dear to the Moslems, with Mecca and Medina.

V. O Lord of compassion;
R. *Sanctify the House of Islam.*

Jerusalem:
City of divided Churches.

V. O Lord of the Church;
R. *Unite us in holiness and love.*

Jerusalem:
Yet to be the city of peace.

V. We pray for thy peace;
R. *O Jerusalem! Jerusalem!*